Ice-Cream

Step by Step Recipes of No Machine Ice-Cream.

MARIA SOBININA

BRILLIANTkitchenideas.com

DEDICATION

This book is dedicated to my beautiful family and friends,
as well as to you, my reader. I am happy to share the
amazing joy of preparing healthy meals with you.

MARIA XOXO

Table of Contents

Vanilla Ice-Cream

INGREDIENTS:

16 Oz **Heavy cream**

10 Oz **Condensed milk**, sweetened

1 teaspoon **Vanilla**, extract, pure

¼ teaspoon **Salt,** pink, Himalayan

EQUIPMENT:

Stand mixer equipped with a whisk attachment, Airtight jar to freeze the ice-cream.

DIRECTIONS:

Step 1: Place the whisk attachment, condensed milk, and heavy cream into the fridge. Leave for one to two hours to cool.

Step 2: In a mixing bowl of a stand mixer add heavy cream. Beat with the whisk attachment on medium speed until cream thickens. Do not overbeat or the cream may turn into butter.

Step 3: Add condensed milk, salt, and vanilla. Beat on medium speed until mixture thickens again.

Place the ice-cream mixture into an airtight jar and leave it in the freezer for at least six hours or overnight.

Serve with fruits or toppings of your choice.

Store Vanilla Ice-Crème in the fridge to up to one month.

Sneakers Ice-Cream

INGREDIENTS:

16 Oz **Heavy cream**

10 Oz **Condensed milk**, sweetened

6 Oz **Peanut butter**

8 **Snickers,** bars, mini

1 teaspoon **Vanilla**, extract, pure

¼ teaspoon **Salt,** pink, Himalayan

EQUIPMENT:

Stand mixer equipped with a whisk attachment, Airtight jar to freeze the ice-cream.

DIRECTIONS:

Step 1: Place the whisk attachment, condensed milk, and heavy cream into the fridge. Leave for one to two hours to cool.

Step 2: In a mixing bowl of a stand mixer add heavy cream. Beat with a whisk attachment, on medium speed, until cream thickens. Do not overbeat, otherwise, the cream may turn into butter.

Step 3: Add condensed milk, salt, and vanilla. Beat

on medium speed until mixture thickens again.

Cut snickers bars onto eight pieces each. Fold in peanut butter and snicker's pieces.

Place the ice-cream mixture into an airtight jar and leave it in the freezer for at least six hours or overnight.

Serve with fruits or toppings of your choice.

Store Sneakers Ice-Crème in the fridge to up to one month.

Cherry Ice-Cream

INGREDIENTS:

16 Oz **Heavy cream**

10 Oz **Condensed milk**, sweetened

12 Oz **Cherries**, dark, sweet, *frozen*

1 teaspoon **Vanilla**, extract, pure

¼ teaspoon **Salt,** pink, Himalayan

EQUIPMENT:

Stand mixer equipped with a whisk attachment, Airtight jar to freeze the ice-cream.

DIRECTIONS:

Step 1: Place the whisk attachment, condensed milk, and heavy cream into the fridge. Leave for one to two hours to cool.

Step 2: In a mixing bowl of a stand mixer add heavy cream. Beat with the whisk attachment on medium speed until cream thickens. Do not overbeat or the cream may turn into butter.

Step 3: Add condensed milk, salt, and vanilla. Beat on medium speed until mixture thickens again.

Step 4: Thaw cherries and stir them into a jelly-like mixture. Fold in cherry jelly into ice-cream mix. Mix evenly.

Place the ice-cream mixture into an airtight jar and leave it in the freezer for at least six hours or overnight.

Serve with fruits or toppings of your choice.

Store Cherry Ice-Crème in the fridge to up to one month.

Pistachio Ice-Cream

INGREDIENTS:

FOR THE ICE-CREAM:

16 Oz **Heavy cream**

10 Oz **Condensed milk**, sweetened

1 teaspoon **Vanilla**, extract, pure

¼ teaspoon **Salt,** pink, Himalayan

FOR THE PISTACHIO PASTE:

4 Oz **Pistachios,** raw

¼ cup **Heavy cream**

½ teaspoon **Lemon**, juice of

EQUIPMENT:

Food processor equipped with S-blade, Stand mixer equipped with a whisk attachment, Airtight jar to freeze the ice-cream.

DIRECTIONS:

MAKE THE PISTACHIO PASTE:

Step 1: In a food processor, combine pistachios with lemon juice and start processing. If the mixture becomes dry, little by little add heavy cream until the mixture becomes a smooth and thick paste. Set aside.

MAKE THE ICE-CREAM:

Step 1: Place the whisk attachment, condensed milk, and heavy cream into the fridge. Leave for one to two hours to cool.

Step 2: In a mixing bowl of a stand mixer add heavy cream. Beat with the whisk attachment on medium speed until cream thickens. Do not overbeat or the cream may turn into butter.

Step 3: Add condensed milk, salt, and vanilla. Beat on medium speed until mixture thickens again.

Fold in pistachio paste.

Place the ice-cream mixture into an airtight jar and leave it in the freezer for at least six hours or overnight.

Serve with fruits or toppings of your choice.

Store Pistachio Ice-Crème in the fridge to up to one month.

Nutella Ice-Cream

INGREDIENTS:

16 Oz **Heavy cream**

8 Oz **Condensed milk**, sweetened

6 Oz **Nutella,** hazelnut spread

1 teaspoon **Vanilla**, extract, pure

¼ teaspoon **Salt,** pink, Himalayan

EQUIPMENT:

Stand mixer equipped with a whisk attachment, Airtight jar to freeze the ice-cream.

DIRECTIONS:

Step 1: Place the whisk attachment, condensed milk, and heavy cream into the fridge. Leave for one to two hours to cool.

Step 2: In a mixing bowl of a stand mixer add heavy cream. Beat with the whisk attachment on medium speed until cream thickens. Do not overbeat or the cream may turn into butter.

Step 3: Add condensed milk, salt, and vanilla. Beat on medium speed until mixture thickens again.

Fold in Nutella spread.

Place the ice-cream mixture into an airtight jar and leave it in the freezer for at least six hours or overnight.

Serve with fruits or toppings of your choice.

Store Nutella Ice-Crème in the fridge to up to one month.

Neapolitan Ice-Cream

INGREDIENTS:

16 Oz **Heavy cream**

10 Oz **Condensed milk**, sweetened

½ cup **Cocoa powder,** raw, unsweetened

8 Oz **Raspberries,** frozen

1 teaspoon **Vanilla**, extract, pure

¼ teaspoon **Salt,** pink, Himalayan

EQUIPMENT:

Stand mixer equipped with a whisk attachment, Airtight jars to freeze the ice-cream.

DIRECTIONS:

Step 1: Place the whisk attachment, condensed milk, and heavy cream into the fridge. Leave for one to two hours to cool.

Step 2: In a mixing bowl of a stand mixer add heavy cream. Beat with the whisk attachment on medium speed until cream thickens. Do not overbeat or the cream may turn into butter.

Step 3: Add condensed milk, salt, and vanilla. Beat

on medium speed until mixture thickens again.

Step 4: Separate the mixture into three parts. Place plain vanilla ice-cream into a jar and place the jar into the freezer.

Mash raspberries with a masher. Fold in raspberries into the second part of the ice-cream mixture. Place into a jar. Place the jar into the freezer.

Fold in cocoa powder into remaining ice-cream, place it into a jar. Place the jar into the freezer. Leave the jars in the freezer for at least six hours or overnight.

Scoop each of the three flavors and serve with toppings of your choice.

Store Neapolitan Ice-Crème in the fridge to up to one month.

Dulce De Leche Ice-Cream

INGREDIENTS:

16 Oz **Heavy cream**

10 Oz **Condensed milk**, sweetened

1 teaspoon **Vanilla**, extract, pure

¼ teaspoon **Salt,** pink, Himalayan

EQUIPMENT:

Small pot, Stand mixer equipped with a whisk attachment, Airtight jar to freeze the ice-cream.

DIRECTIONS:

Step 1: Place the whisk attachment, condensed milk, and heavy cream into the fridge. Leave for one to two hours to cool.

Step 2: Open can of condensed milk. Prepare a water bath by boiling water in a small pot. Place condensed milk in water, covering ½ to ¾ of the can. Cook for about 2 hours, periodically adding more hot water.

The condensed milk will turn caramel in color. This will be your Dulce De Leche.

Step 3: In a mixing bowl of a stand mixer add heavy

cream. Beat with the whisk attachment on medium speed until cream thickens. Do not overbeat or the cream may turn into butter.

Step 4: Add Dulce De Leche, salt, and vanilla. Beat on low-medium speed until mixture thickens again.

Place the ice-cream mixture into an airtight jar and leave it in the freezer for at least six hours or overnight.

Serve with fruits or toppings of your choice.

Store Dulce De Leche Ice-Crème in the fridge to up to one month.

Peppermint Ice-Cream

INGREDIENTS:

16 Oz **Heavy cream**

10 Oz **Condensed milk,** sweetened

½ cup **Mint,** leaves, fresh

1 teaspoon **Peppermint,** extract, pure

1 teaspoon **Vanilla,** extract, pure

¼ teaspoon **Salt,** pink, Himalayan

EQUIPMENT:

Food processor; Stand mixer equipped with a whisk attachment; Airtight jar to freeze the ice-cream.

DIRECTIONS:

Step 1: Place the whisk attachment, condensed milk, and heavy cream into the fridge. Leave for one to two hours to cool.

Step 2: Add ½ cup of heavy cream and mint into a saucepan. Heat and let simmer for five minutes. Set aside to cool. Run it through a mesh strainer to separate mint leaves. Discard the leaves. Place mint cream into the fridge to cool.

Step 3: In a mixing bowl of a stand mixer add heavy cream. Beat with the whisk attachment on medium speed until cream thickens. Do not overbeat or the cream may turn into butter.

Step 4: Add condensed milk, salt, peppermint, and vanilla. Beat on medium speed until mixture thickens again.

Place the ice-cream mixture into an airtight jar and leave it in the freezer for at least six hours or overnight.

Serve with fruits or toppings of your choice.

Store Peppermint Ice-Crème in the fridge to up to one month.

Strawberry Ice-Cream

INGREDIENTS:

16 Oz **Heavy cream**

10 Oz **Condensed milk**, sweetened

12 Oz **Strawberries**, frozen

1 teaspoon **Vanilla**, extract, pure

¼ teaspoon **Salt,** pink, Himalayan

EQUIPMENT:

Stand mixer equipped with a whisk attachment, Airtight jar to freeze the ice-cream.

DIRECTIONS:

Step 1: Place the whisk attachment, condensed milk, and heavy cream into the fridge. Leave for one to two hours to cool.

Step 2: In a mixing bowl of a stand mixer add heavy cream. Beat with the whisk attachment on medium speed until cream thickens. Do not overbeat or the cream may turn into butter.

Step 3: Add condensed milk, salt, and vanilla. Beat on medium speed until mixture thickens again.

Step 4: Thaw strawberries and stir them into a jelly-like mixture. Fold in strawberries jelly into ice-cream mix. Mix evenly.

Place the ice-cream mixture into an airtight jar and leave it in the freezer for at least six hours or overnight.

Serve with fruits or toppings of your choice.

Store Strawberry Ice-Crème in the fridge to up to one month.

Rocky Road Ice-Cream

INGREDIENTS:

16 Oz **Heavy cream**

8 Oz **Condensed milk**, sweetened

6 Oz **Nutella,** hazelnut spread

1 cup **Marshmallow,** mini

1 cup **Walnuts,** raw, chopped

1 cup **Chocolate**, chips, bakers

1 teaspoon **Vanilla**, extract, pure

¼ teaspoon **Salt,** pink, Himalayan

EQUIPMENT:

Stand mixer equipped with a whisk attachment, Airtight jar to freeze the ice-cream.

DIRECTIONS:

Step 1: Place the whisk attachment, condensed milk, and heavy cream into the fridge. Leave for one to two hours to cool.

Step 2: In a mixing bowl of a stand mixer add heavy cream. Beat with the whisk attachment on medium speed until cream thickens. Do not overbeat or the cream may turn into butter.

Step 3: Add condensed milk, salt, and vanilla. Beat on medium speed until mixture thickens again.

Step 4: Prepare a water bath. Melt chocolate chips over the water bath. Set aside to cool for a few minutes.

Fold in Nutella spread, mini marshmallows, chopped walnuts, melted chocolate.

Place the ice-cream mixture into an airtight jar and leave it in the freezer for at least six hours or overnight.

Serve with fruits or toppings of your choice.

Store Rocky Road Ice-Crème in the fridge to up to one month.

Mango Ice-Cream

INGREDIENTS:

16 Oz **Heavy cream**

10 Oz **Condensed milk**, sweetened

1 **Mango**, fresh

1 teaspoon **Vanilla**, extract, pure

¼ teaspoon **Salt,** pink, Himalayan

EQUIPMENT:

Stand mixer equipped with a whisk attachment, Airtight jar to freeze the ice-cream.

DIRECTIONS:

Step 1: Place the whisk attachment, condensed milk, and heavy cream into the fridge. Leave for one to two hours to cool.

Step 2: In a mixing bowl of a stand mixer add heavy cream. Beat with the whisk attachment on medium speed until cream thickens. Do not overbeat or the cream may turn into butter.

Step 3: Add condensed milk, salt, and vanilla. Beat on medium speed until mixture thickens again.

Step 4: Peel mangos, separate meat from the pit. Puree mango meat and fold it into the ice-cream mix. Mix evenly.

Place the ice-cream mixture into an airtight jar and leave it in the freezer for at least six hours or overnight.

Serve with fruits or toppings of your choice.

Store Mango Ice-Crème in the fridge to up to one month.

Oreo Cookies Ice-Cream

INGREDIENTS:

16 Oz **Heavy cream**

10 Oz **Condensed milk**, sweetened

2 cups **Oreo cookies,** crumbled

1 teaspoon **Vanilla**, extract, pure

¼ teaspoon **Salt,** pink, Himalayan

EQUIPMENT:

Food processor or Rolling pin, Stand mixer equipped with a whisk attachment, Airtight jar to freeze the ice-cream.

DIRECTIONS:

Place cookies in a food processor and pulse until cookies are crumbled. Alternatively, place cookies in to a plastic bag and crumble using a rolling pin.

Step 1: Place cookies into a food processor and pulse until the cookies are crumbled. Alternatively, place cookies into a plastic bag and crumble the cookies using a rolling pin.

Step 2: In a mixing bowl of a stand mixer add heavy cream. Beat with the whisk attachment on medium speed until cream thickens. Do not overbeat or the cream may turn into butter.

Step 3: Add condensed milk, salt, and vanilla. Beat on medium speed until mixture thickens again.

Fold in Oreo cookies and mix evenly.

Place the ice-cream mixture into an airtight jar and leave it in the freezer for at least six hours or overnight.

Serve with fruits or toppings of your choice.

Store Oreo Cookies Ice-Crème in the fridge to up to one month.

Blueberry Ice-Cream

INGREDIENTS:

16 Oz **Heavy cream**

10 Oz **Condensed milk**, sweetened

12 Oz **Blueberries**, frozen

1 teaspoon **Vanilla**, extract, pure

¼ teaspoon **Salt,** pink, Himalayan

EQUIPMENT:

Stand mixer equipped with a whisk attachment, Airtight jar to freeze the ice-cream.

DIRECTIONS:

Step 1: Place the whisk attachment, condensed milk, and heavy cream into the fridge. Leave for one to two hours to cool.

Step 2: In a mixing bowl of a stand mixer add heavy cream. Beat with the whisk attachment on medium speed until cream thickens. Do not overbeat or the cream may turn into butter.

Step 3: Add condensed milk, salt, and vanilla. Beat on medium speed until mixture thickens again.

Step 4: Thaw blueberries and stir into jelly-like mixture. Fold in blueberries jelly into ice-cream mix. Mix evenly.

Place the ice-cream mixture into an airtight jar and leave it in the freezer for at least six hours or overnight.

Serve with fruits or toppings of your choice.

Store Blueberry Ice-Crème in the fridge to up to one month.

Choco-Nut Ice-Cream

INGREDIENTS:

FOR THE ICE-CREAM:

16 Oz **Heavy cream**

10 Oz **Condensed milk**, sweetened

½ cup **Cocoa powder**, Dutch, processed

1 teaspoon **Vanilla**, extract, pure

¼ teaspoon **Salt,** pink, Himalayan

FOR THE NUT PASTE:

4 Oz **Pistachios,** raw

4 Oz **Walnuts,** raw

4 Oz **Brazilian nuts,** raw

¼ cup **Heavy cream**

½ teaspoon **Lemon**, juice of

EQUIPMENT:

Food processor equipped with S-blade, Stand mixer equipped with a whisk attachment, Airtight jar to freeze the ice-cream.

DIRECTIONS:

MAKE THE NUT PASTE:

Step 1: In a food processor, combine all one-half of all nuts with lemon juice and start processing. If the mixture becomes dry, little by little add heavy cream until the mixture becomes a smooth and thick paste. Set aside. Chop other half nuts into small pieces.

MAKE THE ICE-CREAM:

Step 1: Place the whisk attachment, condensed milk, and heavy cream into the fridge. Leave for one to two hours to cool.

Step 2: In a mixing bowl of a stand mixer add heavy cream. Beat with the whisk attachment on medium speed until cream thickens. Do not overbeat or the cream may turn into butter.

Step 3: Add condensed milk, salt, cocoa powder, and vanilla. Beat on low-medium speed until mixture thickens again.

Fold in nut paste and chopped nuts. Mix evenly.

Place the ice-cream mixture into an airtight jar and leave it in the freezer for at least six hours or overnight.

Serve with fruits or toppings of your choice.

Store Choco Nut Ice-Crème in the fridge to up to one month.

Black Forest Meringue Ice-Cream

INGREDIENTS:

FOR THE ICE-CREAM:

16 Oz **Heavy cream**

10 Oz **Condensed milk**, sweetened

12 Oz **Cherries**, dark, sweet, *frozen*

½ cup **Cocoa powder**, Dutch, processed

1 teaspoon **Vanilla**, extract, pure

¼ teaspoon **Salt,** pink, Himalayan

FOR THE MERINGUE:

4 **Eggs whites,** room temperature

1 cup **Sugar,** white, granulated

1/3 teaspoon **Cream of tartar**

1 teaspoon **Vanilla,** pure, extract

EQUIPMENT:

Food processor, Stand mixer equipped with a whisk attachment, Baking tray, Pastry bag, Decorating tip with a small hole, Airtight jar to freeze the ice-cream, Parchment paper.

DIRECTIONS:

MAKE THE MERINGUE:

Preheat the oven to 250°.

Step 1: In a bowl of stand mixer fitted with the paddle attachment combine egg whites, cream of tartar, vanilla. Beat on medium speed until foamy.

One spoon at a time, add sugar and beat until sugar dissolves, then add more sugar. Repeat. Continue beating for 7 to 10 minutes until still glossy peaks start forming.

Step 2: Take a pastry bag and set a decorating tip with a small hole. Alternatively, you can cut a small hole in the pastry piping bag.

Step 3: Transfer meringue to the piping bag. Pipe 1 ½ – 2-inch diameter cookies onto a large baking tray lined with parchment paper. Space them 2 inches apart.

Step 4: Bake meringues on a large tray for 40-45 minutes or until they become firm.

Turn off oven and leave meringues in the oven for about one hour.

Step 5: Remove meringues from the oven, separate from the parchment paper. Set aside small meringues for cake decorations.

Place meringues into a plastic bag and turn them into crumbs using a rolling pin. Set aside.

MAKE THE ICE-CREAM:

Step 1: Place the whisk attachment, condensed milk, and heavy cream into the fridge. Leave for one to two hours to cool.

Step 2: In a mixing bowl of a stand mixer add heavy cream. Beat with the whisk attachment on medium speed until cream thickens. Do not overbeat or the cream may turn into butter.

Step 3: Add condensed milk, cocoa powder, salt, and vanilla. Beat on medium speed until the mixture thickens again.

Step 4: Thaw cherries and stir them into a jelly-like mixture. Fold in cherry jelly and meringue crumbs into ice-cream mix. Mix evenly.

Place the ice-cream mixture into an airtight jar and leave it in the freezer for at least six hours or overnight.

Serve with fruits or toppings of your choice.

Store Black Forest Meringue Ice-Crème in the fridge to up to one month.

Lemon Lime Ice-Cream

INGREDIENTS:

16 Oz **Heavy cream**

10 Oz **Condensed milk**, sweetened

12 Oz **Blueberries**, frozen

½ **Lemon**, juice of

½ **Lime**, juice of

1 teaspoon **Vanilla**, extract, pure

¼ teaspoon **Salt,** pink, Himalayan

EQUIPMENT:

Food processor, Stand mixer equipped with a whisk attachment, Airtight jar to freeze the ice-cream.

DIRECTIONS:

Step 1: Place the whisk attachment, condensed milk, and heavy cream into the fridge. Leave for one to two hours to cool.

Step 2: In a mixing bowl of a stand mixer add heavy cream. Beat with the whisk attachment on medium speed until cream thickens. Do not overbeat or the cream may turn into butter.

Step 3: Add condensed milk, juices of lemon and lime, salt, and vanilla. Beat on medium speed until mixture thickens again.

Place the ice-cream mixture into an airtight jar and leave it in the freezer for at least six hours or overnight.

Serve with fruits or toppings of your choice.

Store Lemon Lime Ice-Crème in the fridge to up to one month.

Coconut Ice-Cream

INGREDIENTS:

FOR THE ICE-CREAM:

16 Oz **Heavy cream**

10 Oz **Condensed milk**, sweetened

½ cup **Coconut,** shredded, unsweetened

1 teaspoon **Vanilla**, extract, pure

¼ teaspoon **Salt,** pink, Himalayan

For the Nut Paste:

1 cup **Coconut,** shredded, unsweetened

1 teaspoon **Lemon,** juice of

1 cup **Water**

EQUIPMENT:

Food processor equipped with S-blade, Stand mixer equipped with a whisk attachment, Airtight jar to freeze the ice-cream.

DIRECTIONS:

MAKE THE COCONUT PASTE:

Step 1: In a food processor, combine shredded

coconut with lemon juice and start processing. If the mixture becomes dry, little by little add water until the mixture becomes a smooth and thick paste. Set aside.

MAKE THE ICE-CREAM:

Step 1: Place the whisk attachment, condensed milk, and heavy cream into the fridge. Leave for one to two hours to cool.

Step 2: In a mixing bowl of a stand mixer add heavy cream. Beat with the whisk attachment on medium speed until cream thickens. Do not overbeat or the cream may turn into butter.

Step 3: Add condensed milk, salt, and vanilla. Beat on low-medium speed until mixture thickens again.

Fold in coconut paste and shredded coconut. Mix evenly.

Place the ice-cream mixture into an airtight jar and leave it in the freezer for at least six hours or overnight.

Serve with fruits or toppings of your choice.

Store Coconut Ice-Crème in the fridge to up to one month.

Thank You for Purchasing This Book!

I create and test recipes for you. I hope you enjoyed these recipes.

Your review of this book helps me succeed & grow. If you enjoyed this book, please leave me a short (1-2 sentence) review on Amazon.

Thank you so much for reviewing this book!

Do you have any questions?
Email me at: **Maria@BRILLIANTkithenideas.com**

**MARIA SOBININA
BRILLIANT kitchen ideas**

Would you like to learn cooking techniques and tips? Visit us at:

www. BRILLIANTkitchenideas.com